Smithsonian

Star Power

Amy Pastan and Linda McKnight

Star

Smithsonian
Power

Collins
An Imprint of HarperCollinsPublishers

HarperCollins books may be purchased for educational, business, or sales promotional use. For information please write: Special Markets Department, HarperCollins Publishers, 10 East 53rd Street, New York, NY 10022.

FIRST EDITION

Designed by Linda McKnight, McKnight Design, LLC
Edited by Anita Schwartz

The authors would like to thank Ellen Nanney of Smithsonian Business Ventures for coordinating this project. Her efforts made this book series possible.

Library of Congress Cataloging-in-Publication Data has been applied for.

ISBN 978-0-06-125152-8

07 08 09 10 11   TP   10 9 8 7 6 5 4 3 2 1

The authors would like to thank the following Smithsonian museums, research centers, and offices for their assistance and cooperation in the making of Spotlight Smithsonian books:

Anacostia Community Museum
Archives of American Art
Arthur M. Sackler Gallery
Cooper-Hewitt, National Design Museum
Freer Gallery of Art
Hirshhorn Museum and Sculpture Garden
National Air and Space Museum
National Air and Space Museum's
    Steven F. Udvar-Hazy Center
National Anthropology Archives
National Museum of African Art
National Museum of American History,
    Kenneth E. Behring Center
National Museum of the American Indian
National Museum of Natural History
National Portrait Gallery
National Postal Museum
National Zoological Park
Smithsonian American Art Museum
    and its Renwick Gallery
Smithsonian Institution Libraries
Smithsonian Institution Archives
Smithsonian Astrophysical Observatory
Smithsonian Center for Folklife
    and Cultural Heritage
Smithsonian Environmental Research Center
Smithsonian Photographic Services
Smithsonian Tropical Research Institute
Smithsonian Women's Committee,
    Office of Development

Smithsonian Star Power

Where can you see screen stars Marilyn Monroe, Katharine Hepburn, Ingrid Bergman, and Rudolph Valentino, sports stars Arthur Ashe, Muhammad Ali, and Jackie Robinson, music stars John Lennon and Bob Dylan, "Star Dust" sheet music, and one of the largest star rubies in the world? From rock stars to movie stars—the Smithsonian has it all. But with seventeen museums and a zoo in Washington, D.C., two museums in New York City, various research centers, and more than 137 million objects in all, the Smithsonian can be overwhelming—even for those who have the opportunity to come often. *Smithsonian Star Power* offers a selection of unique items from the collections and allows you to see them as no other visitor can. In these pages you can experience highlights from the exhibits as well as see lesser-known materials that are seldom on view. For those with stars in their eyes, Celia Cruz's *bata cubana*, Ray Charles' sunglasses, Marilyn Monroe's lips, and Prince's Yellow Cloud guitar will inspire awe. Explore distant galaxies photographed at the Smithsonian Astrophysical Observatory as well as Asian star imagery at the Freer and Sackler Galleries. Enjoy the world's largest museum, cultural, and scientific complex without planning a trip and fighting the crowds. Reach for the stars, and return as often as you like.

Celia Cruz Bata Cubana

Designed by Enrique Arteaga
Polyester satin trimmed with insertion lace,
interwoven with orange ribbon
National Museum of American History
Division of Music, Sports, and Entertainment
Gift of The Celia Cruz Foundation, 1997

Marilyn Monroe's Lips

1962
Andy Warhol
Synthetic polymer, silkscreen ink and pencil
on canvas
Hirshhorn Museum and Sculpture Garden
Gift of Joseph H. Hirshhorn, 1972
©Andy Warhol Foundation for the Visual
Arts/ARS, New York
™ 2007 Marilyn Monroe, LLC by CMG
Worldwide, Inc.

Pop artist Andy Warhol (1928-1987)
based this image of Marilyn Monroe's
lips on a publicity still made for her
1953 film *Niagara*. Fascinated by
Americans' fixation on celebrities such
as the glamorous blonde film star, the
artist began a series of portraits of her
shortly after her death in 1962. Like
many of Warhol's subjects, Marilyn
served as a symbol of the public's
dreams and desires.

August 11, 1967, London, England
Made for Richard Avedon Posters, Inc.
Richard Avedon
Published by Cowles Education Corporation
Offset lithograph on white wove paper
Cooper-Hewitt, National Design Museum
Gift of Various Donors
Courtesy The Richard Avedon Foundation
©1967 The Richard Avedon Foundation

A quintessential image of the psychedelic era of the 1960s, this poster by Richard Avedon is of Beatle John Lennon, then in his "Sgt. Pepper" phase. The highly saturated orange, red, and yellow seem to suit Lennon's bold personality and the glasses with lenses formed by bright orange, green, and white spirals draw the viewer's attention to Lennon's trademark wire rims. This is one of a series of posters featuring the Beatles that Avedon sold through *Look* magazine.

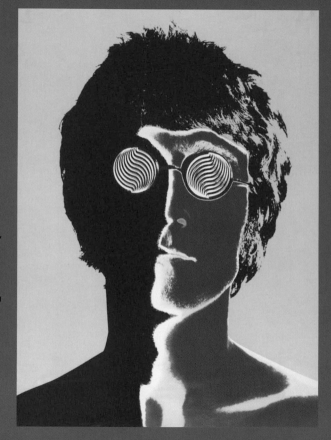

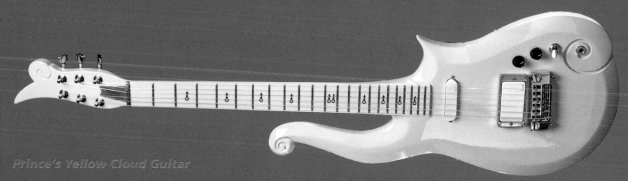

Prince's Yellow Cloud Guitar

1989
National Museum of American History
Division of Music, Sports, and Entertainment
Gift of Paisley Park Enterprises

The distinctive shape and vibrant yellow of Prince's (b. 1958) guitar reflect the musician's innovative music and flamboyant style. Prince designed the instrument—called the Yellow Cloud— using his personal icon, a combination of the male and female symbols, for the fingerboard inlays. The guitar was custom-built by Minneapolis craftsmen. An icon in his own right, Prince is a remarkably prolific and versatile superstar, who composes, arranges, and performs his own songs.

Bob Dylan

1965
Lisa Law
Gelatin silver print
National Museum of American History
Division of Information Technology
and Communications
Photographic History Collection
© Lisa Law

In the early 1960s, Lisa Law worked as personal assistant to the manager of The Kingston Trio. He gave her a camera and asked her to photograph musicians for his record company. This gave Law the extraordinary opportunity to meet and take images of many of the artists whose work defined a generation. Some, like Bob Dylan, visited Law's southern California home, called "The Castle," which became a haven for counterculture celebrities.

The Bubbler
Wurlitzer Jukebox, Model 1015

1946
Made by Wurlitzer Co.
North Tonawanda, NY
National Museum of American History
Division of Music, Sports, and Entertainment
Gift of Roth Novelty Co.

Rudolph Wurlitzer, born in 1829, emigrated to America from Germany at the age of twenty-four and founded a music company in Ohio. At first he imported instruments from his homeland, but by the late 1880s he began manufacturing novelty music products, such as the coin-operated electric piano, which appeared in 1896. Rudolph's successors moved the company to New York State and continued his innovative work. This bubbler jukebox, released by Wurlitzer just after World War II, was enormously popular. With its visible record changer and colored bubble tubes, it is considered a classic.

Yo-Yo Ma at the Smithsonian Folklife Festival

Smithsonian Folklife Festival 2002
Harold Dorwin
Color photograph
Smithsonian Center for Folklife and
Cultural Heritage

Star cellist Yo-Yo Ma plays on camera at the Smithsonian Folklife Festival 2002, with an appreciative camel for an audience. That year, the Festival celebrated the Silk Road, an ancient network of trade routes that brought ideas, culture, music, and art across the mountains and deserts of Central Asia, connecting East Asia and the Mediterranean.

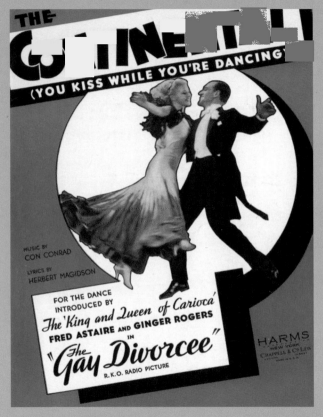

"The Continental" from The Gay Divorcee

1934
Sheet music
Archives Center, National Museum of American History
Sam DeVincent Collection of Illustrated American Sheet Music
™ 2007 Ginger Rogers by CMG Worldwide, Inc.

Who could "step out" better than dancers Fred Astaire and Ginger Rogers? This sheet music for "The Continental" from the RKO motion picture *Gay Divorcee* shows the pair in midair. This romantic comedy was released in 1934 and won three Academy Award nominations. "The Continental," a twenty-two minute production number, won an Oscar for best song.

"Rudolph Valentino Blues"

1922
Sheet music
Archives Center, National Museum of
American History
Sam DeVincent Collection of Illustrated
American Sheet Music

The Sam DeVincent Collection of
Illustrated American Sheet Music is filled
with stars. One example pictured here
shows heart-throb Rudolph Valentino
on the cover of "Rudolph Valentino
Blues" from 1922. Valentino (1895-
1926) starred in several popular films
including *The Eagle* (1925) and *Son of
the Sheik* (1926) before his untimely
death at the age of thirty-one. His
performances continue to impress fans
of early film.

Janis Joplin and Big Brother and the Holding Company

1967
Lisa Law
Gelatin silver print
National Museum of American History
Division of Information Technology
and Communications
Photographic History Collection
© Lisa Law

Wild, Bohemian, tough, and talented—
singer Janis Joplin (1943-1970)
was all of these things. Her reckless
bluesy voice made her a star but her
participation in the psychedelic drug
culture of the 1960s brought her to an
early death. At a time when few women
were in rock bands, Joplin was asked
to join Big Brother and the Holding
Company as lead singer. The group was
well-known in San Francisco's hippie
community.

The Wild Bunch

1900
John Swartz
Gelatin silver print
National Portrait Gallery
Gift of Pinkerton's, Inc.

Butch Cassidy is the alias of Robert LeRoy Parker, born in 1865 (sitting bottom right) in Utah. He left home at an early age and worked on several ranches before becoming the mastermind of train robberies and bank heists that made him a living legend. Charming and brave, Cassidy attracted other famous outlaws to assist in his schemes. His band, called the Wild Bunch, included the Sundance Kid (seated left), the Tall Texan (seated center), Bill Carver (standing left) and Harvey Logan (standing right).

Celia Cruz Bata Cubana

Designed by Enrique Arteaga
Polyester satin trimmed with insertion lace,
interwoven with orange ribbon
National Museum of American History
Division of Music, Sports, and Entertainment
Gift of The Celia Cruz Foundation, 1997

The National Museum of American
History celebrated the life of the
legendary queen of Latin music,
Celia Cruz (1925-2003) in a popular
exhibition that highlighted important
moments in her career. Through
photographs, documents, videos, and
sound recordings, "Azúcar: The Life and
Music of Celia Cruz" was a big hit. Of
special interest to visitors were Cruz's
extravagant costumes, such as this
orange *bata cubana*, which the salsa
queen wore first at Carnegie Hall and
later at the Apollo Theater.

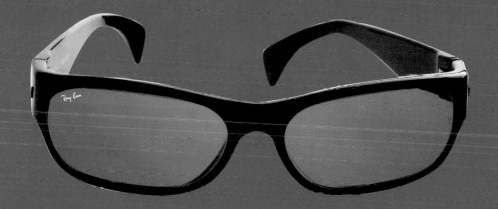

Ray Charles Sunglasses

National Museum of American History
Division of Music, Sports, and Entertainment

Born into poverty and blinded by glaucoma at age seven, Ray Charles rose to stardom, gaining worldwide recognition as a singer, composer, and pianist. His gravelly voice and his genius for working in diverse genres—from country and jazz to soul—won him respect and admiration across generations. The Smithsonian has personal items that belonged to Ray Charles in the collections of the National Museum of American History, including his trademark Ray-Ban™ sunglasses.

"Mother Goose's Star Rhymes"

Schultz & Co.
Star Soap booklet
Archives Center, National Museum of
American History
Warshaw Collection of Business Americana,
c. 1724-1977

This pamphlet was produced to
market Star Soap. Isadore Warshaw, a
newspaper publisher/publicist, collected
ephemera like this which can now be
seen in the Warshaw Collection of
Business Americana at the Archives
Center, National Museum of American
History. Fascinating for visitors and
important to researchers, the posters,
labels, invoices, ads, calendars, business
cards and correspondence in the archive
are an invaluable resource for those
documenting the history of business in
America, as well as the general history
of the nation itself. From soap to steel,
there are many treasures among the
1,020 cubic feet of material.

Marilyn Monroe

1954
David D. Geary
Color positive transparency
National Portrait Gallery
Gift of David Geary
™ 2007 Marilyn Monroe, LLC by CMG
Worldwide, Inc.

One of the brightest stars in Hollywood in 1954 had to have been Marilyn Monroe (1926-1962). Imagine the scene when Monroe arrived in Korea to entertain the troops stationed there— pandemonium. Among the soldiers vying for a look at the blond bombshell was Navy Hospitalman Second Class David Geary. Because of his Red Cross armband, Geary was mistaken for a doctor and commissioned officer and given a second row seat with a perfect view of the stage. This is one of the shots he took as Monroe cast her spell on the audience.

United States, 20 Dollars, 1849 (pattern)

1849
Designer: J. Longacre
Maker: U.S. Mint
National Museum of American History
Numismatics, Division of Information
Technology and Communications

Stars adorn this twenty dollar coin from 1849. Made at the height of the Gold Rush, when the precious metal was abundant, it was one of two gold denominations produced that year; the other was a tiny gold dollar. James B. Longacre, the artist, executed the design of the coin for the U.S. Mint. The National Numismatics Collection at the National Museum of American History houses rare and valuable examples of U.S. coinage and currency.

Arthur Ashe

1993
Louis Briel
Acrylic on canvas
National Portrait Gallery
Gift of the Commonwealth of Virginia and
Virginia's Heroes, Inc.
™ 2007 Arthur Ashe, Inc. by CMG
Worldwide, Inc.

This portrait, made in 1993, the year
of Arthur Ashe's death (1943-1993),
depicts the three-time Grand Slam
winner in business attire, resting
his hands on a tennis racket poised
between his legs. His dress may seem
irregular for a sports celebrity, but
Ashe—the first African American
selected to the U.S. Davis Cup Team—
had a serious side and a great social
conscience. He protested the practice
of apartheid in South Africa in the late
1960s and early 1970s and used his
own sad history with HIV—contracted
from blood transfusions he received
during heart surgery—to call attention
to those suffering from AIDS worldwide.

"As Time Goes By" from Casablanca

1931
Sheet music
Archives Center, National Museum of
American History
Sam DeVincent Collection of Illustrated
American Sheet Music
™ 2007 Ingrid Bergman by CMG Worldwide,
Inc.
Humphrey Bogart © & ™, Bogart Inc., c/o
Licensebox, A Moda Entertainment Inc.
Company

The performance of Herman Hupfeld's
song "As Time Goes By" is one of the
most memorable moments—and there
are many—in the 1942 film *Casablanca*,
starring Humphrey Bogart as an
American expatriate club owner and
Ingrid Bergman as Ilsa Lund, his ex-lover.
These stars pull off an unforgettable
performance, leading some critics to
place *Casablanca* on the list of greatest
films of all time. "As Time Goes By"
was actually first performed in the 1931
musical "Everybody's Welcome."

"Star Dust"

1929
Sheet music
Archives Center, National Museum of
American History
Sam DeVincent Collection of Illustrated
American Sheet Music

"Star Dust," is an enduring standard by one of America's greatest composers— Hoagy Carmichael, whose songs are among the most memorable of the twentieth century. "Star Dust" has been recorded more than 1,600 times and translated into thirty languages. Carmichael (1899–1981) had a law degree from Indiana University but was lured away from that career by his love of jazz. His other well-known compositions include "Georgia on My Mind," Rockin' Chair," and "Lazy River."

Ali Jumping Rope

1966
Gordon Parks
Gelatin silver print
Smithsonian American Art Museum
Museum purchase through the Horace W.
Goldsmith Foundation
© The Gordon Parks Foundation, All Rights
Reserved
Courtesy Howard Greenberg Gallery, NYC

Photographer Gordon Parks (1912-
2006) took this image of world-renown
sports luminary Muhammad Ali (b.
1942). Ali brought extraordinary speed
and a graceful style to boxing. His two
fights with Sonny Liston, bouts with Joe
Frazier, victory over George Foreman,
and defeat of Leon Spinks earned him
the self-proclaimed title "The Greatest."
Born Cassius Clay, Jr., Ali changed his
name when he embraced Islam. He has
devoted much of his life to charitable
and humanitarian causes.

The Seaside

c. 1955
Joseph Cornell
Printed papers, colored sand, driftwood,
coral, nut, starfish, glass, and marbles, in
glass-faced wood box
Hishhorn Museum and Sculpture Garden
The Joseph H. Hirshhorn Bequest, 1981
Art © The Joseph and Robert Cornell
Memorial Foundation, Licensed by VAGA,
New York, NY

American artist Joseph Cornell (1903-1972) is perhaps best-known for his boxed assemblages constructed with found objects. These glass-fronted cases, usually filled with photographs and bric-a-brac, reveal the lively influence of surrealism on the artist, although Cornell never called himself a surrealist. This example of his work at the Hirshhorn Museum and Sculpture Garden is an amusing seaside in a box, complete with starfish.

Hooked Rug with Stars, Crescent and Fret

After 1850
Unidentified
Wool on burlap
Smithsonian American Art Museum
Gift of Herbert Waide Hemphill, Jr. and
museum purchase made possible by Ralph
Cross Johnson

Hooked rugs, in which unknotted loops of yarn, fabric scraps, or ribbon were pulled through a coarse stretched backing, became popular in the 1850s. Later, mass-produced stencils were available for patterns. This rug, however, does not appear to be based on any commercially available pattern. The red, white, blue, and gray colors suggest a patriotic motif, interpreted by some as a representation of the Confederacy. It is more probable, however, that the rug maker was creating an original design without reference to any historic event.

The American Indian

1970
Fritz Scholder (Luiseño)
Oil on linen
National Museum of the American Indian
Indian Arts and Crafts Board Collection,
Department of the Interior

Draped in the stars and stripes designed
as a Native blanket, this Indian holds a
feathered tomahawk and appears to be
laughing. Seen by some as an emblem
of patriotism, the painting is interpreted
by others as a protest against unfair
treatment of Indians by the U.S.
government in the 1960s and 1970s.
This enigmatic work was created by Fritz
Scholder. His accomplishments helped
gain status for a whole generation of
Native artists.

P.T. Barnum and General Tom Thumb

c. 1850
Samuel Root and Marcus Aurelius Root
Daguerreotype
National Portrait Gallery

Showman P.T. Barnum discovered Charles Stratton in 1842. Stratton was five years old at the time, but weighed only fifteen pounds and stood only twenty five inches tall. Barnum trained the child to sing and dance, renamed him "Tom Thumb" and billed him as an eleven-year-old wonder. The act was enormously popular and Barnum took "Tom" on a worldwide tour to perform for queens, kings, and other dignitaries.

Apollo-Soyuz Mission Patch

1975
National Air and Space Museum

The Apollo-Soyuz Test Project docked an American Apollo and a Soviet Soyuz spacecraft in orbit in July 1975. Soviet crewmembers Alexsei Leonov and Valerii Kubasov joined Americans Thomas Stafford, Deke Slayton, and Vance Brand for the first international space mission, via the jointly designed docking adapter airlock. Both Soviet and U.S. crews wore this star-adorned mission patch.

ATTACKED
BY THE
GIANT
REPTILE

Buck Rogers, 25th century,
featuring Buddy and Allura
in "Strange Adventures in
the Spider Ship"

Dick Calkins (1895-1962)
c. 1935
Chicago: Pleasure Books
Smithsonian Institution Libraries

Buck Rogers originated in 1928 as
Anthony Rogers, the hero of two
novellas by Philip Francis Nowlon. He
has since become a cultural icon in the
science fiction world, starring in a comic
strip, movie serial, a television series, a
computer game, and in this whimsical
pop-up book housed in the Smithsonian
Institution Libraries. Buck's adventures in
outer space became an important part
of American pop culture and introduced
the concept of space exploration to
a broad audience. His swashbuckling
adventures among the stars continue to
fascinate adults and children.

Amelia Earhart with a Lockheed Electra and Cord Phaeton

September 20, 1936
J.C. Allen
Gelatin silver print
National Air and Space Museum Archives
Courtesy of Purdue University, from Purdue University Libraries' The George Palmer Putnam Collection of Amelia Earhart Papers
™ 2007 Amelia Earhart by CMG Worldwide, Inc.

With her spirit for adventure, self-confidence, and charm, aviator Amelia Earhart (1897-1937) won over many of her critics, who felt women were not suited to piloting airplanes. Earhart proved them wrong when she became the first person to fly solo from Hawaii to California in 1935. Two years later, she attempted a flight around the world, but disappeared over the Pacific Ocean in July 1937. Her Lockheed Vega airplane is in the collection of the National Air and Space Museum.

Pan American Airways Travel Poster

n.d.
Gelatin silver print photograph of poster
National Air and Space Museum Archives

This travel poster dates from the golden age of commercial aviation in the 1930s. The Pan American fleet—called "clippers"—were actually planes named after sailing ships from the nineteenth century. Pan Am's crews wore naval-style uniforms that bore naval ranks. With the stars and stripes for its backdrop, a Boeing 377 Stratocruiser flies around the world.

Charles Lindbergh with Ryan NYP, " Spirit of St. Louis"

c. 1927
Unidentified photographer
Toned gelatin silver print
National Air and Space Museum Archives

Charles Lindbergh, who made the first nonstop solo flight across the Atlantic Ocean on May 20-21, 1927, earned international fame for his feat. Nicknamed "Lucky Lindy" by the press, he was idolized by Americans and Europeans. The airplane Lindbergh flew from New York to Paris—the *Spirit of St. Louis*—is in the collection of the National Air and Space Museum.

General George S. Patton, Jr.

1945
Boleslaw Jan Czedekowski
Oil on canvas
National Portrait Gallery
Gift of Major General George S. Patton, USA
Retired and the Patton Family
™ 2007 General George S. Patton, Jr., by
CMG Worldwide, Inc.

General George S. Patton (1885-1945),
looking every bit the warrior in this formal
portrait, deserved his stars. A leading U.S.
Army general during World War II, he
had a thirty-six year career in the military.
Patton commanded major units in North
Africa, Sicily, and the European Theater
of Operations during the war. Often
criticized for his ruthless style, he was also
recognized as a brilliant military strategist.

- BING CROSBY
- BOB HOPE
- FRED MacMURRAY
- FRANCHOT TONE
- RAY MILLAND
- VICTOR MOORE
- DOROTHY LAMOUR
- PAULETTE GODDARD
- VERA ZORINA
- MARY MARTIN
- DICK POWELL
- BETTY HUTTON
- EDDIE BRACKEN
- VERONICA LAKE
- ALAN LADD
- ROCHESTER

- WILLIAM BENDIX
- JERRY COLONNA
- MACDONALD CAREY
- WALTER ABEL
- SUSAN HAYWARD
- MARJORIE REYNOLDS
- BETTY RHODES
- DONA DRAKE
- LYNNE OVERMAN
- GARY CROSBY
- JOHNNIE JOHNSTON
- GIL LAMB
- CASS DALEY
- ERNEST TRUEX
- KATHERINE DUNHAM
- ARTHUR TREACHER
- WALTER CATLETT
- STERLING HOLLOWAY
- GOLDEN GATE QUARTETTE
- WALTER DARE WAHL AND COMPANY
- CECIL B. DeMILLE
- PRESTON STURGES
- RALPH MURPHY

Directed by George Marshall
Original Screen Play by Harry Tugend
A Paramount Picture

Star-Spangled Rhythm
Lobby Card

1942
National Museum of American History
Division of Military History and Diplomacy

Lobby cards, smaller in size than posters, were once mounted in theater display cases to advertise movies. This lobby card for the film *Star-Spangled Rhythm* reads like a "Who's Who" of stars from the 1930s and 1940s—Victor Moore, Bob Hope, Franchot Tore, Dorothy Lamour, Veronica Lake, Paulette Goddard, Alan Ladd, Bing Crosby, Cecil B. DeMille, Preston Sturges, and others.

Jackie Robinson, outfield, Brooklyn Dodgers

Jackie Robinson Baseball Card, No. 10

1954
Published by Topps
National Museum of American History
Division of Music, Sports, and Entertainment
TM 2007 Rachel Robinson by CMG
Worldwide, Inc.

Legendary baseball player Jackie Robinson (1919-1972) debuted with the Brooklyn Dodgers in 1947, breaking the "color line" in the major leagues. This Topps baseball card from 1954 shows the star at the top of his game. In that year he became the first National Leaguer to steal his way around the bases. In ten seasons, Robinson helped the Dodgers win six pennants, where he dominated the game by stealing home nineteen times.

Star

1985
Robert Cottingham
Color lithograph
Smithsonian American Art Museum
Gift of an anonymous donor

Internationally recognized as one of America's most important photo-realist painters, Robert Cottingham (b. 1935) studied advertising and graphic design at Pratt Institute in New York from 1959 to 1963. After graduating, he was employed as an art director at advertising agencies, but eventually began to paint every day after work. His earliest works are of the same style, character, and subject matter for which he is known: precisely rendered images of neon signs, architectural details, storefronts, and other elements of the American urban landscape.

The Star Columns

February 24–August 25, 1889
Charles M. Kurtz
Scrapbook
Archives of American Art
Charles M. Kurtz Papers, 1843–1990

While Charles M. Kurtz may not be a household name, his papers at the Archives of American Art are of importance because he was a prominent figure in American art in the last quarter of the nineteenth and first quarter of the twentieth centuries. Known for his critical writings about art—such as those for the *New York Daily Star* collected in this scrapbook—he is also remembered for his accomplishments as arts administrator at the 1893 Columbian Exposition in Chicago, as well as for serving as first director of the Albright-Knox Gallery in Buffalo, New York.

Hollywood

1965
Red Grooms
Construction of acrylic on wood, metal foil,
nails, and plaster
Hirshhorn Museum and Sculpture Garden
Gift of Joseph H. Hirshhorn, 1972
© 2007 Red Grooms/Artists Rights Society
(ARS), New York

Red Grooms (b. 1937) is a multimedia
artist known for his colorful constructions,
usually involving cartoon-like characters
in the modern urban landscape. This
Hollywood scene is a throwback to the
golden age of the screen, when female
actresses dramatically threw themselves
into the arms of their handsome co-stars.
Early in his career, Grooms made several
short films of his own. He is also a prolific
printmaker.

Egret against Night Sky

n.d.
Ohara Koson (Shoson) 1877-1945
Japanese
Woodblock print, ink and color on paper
Robert O. Muller Collection
Arthur M. Sackler Gallery of Art

Within the Robert O. Muller Collection
at the Arthur M. Sackler Gallery there
are more than 200 Japanese artists'
works represented and more than 400
examples by bird-and-flower specialist
Ohara Koson, who created this elegant
egret against a star-studded sky.
The snow-covered branch gracefully
descending from the top left corner
of the image to the lower right, the
white bird perched on one foot, and
the delicately twinkling stars against a
black sky are all simple but powerful
components of the composition.

Fanny Brice

1918
Alfred Cheney Johnston
Platinum print
National Portrait Gallery

Born Fania Borach on the Lower East
Side in New York City, Fanny Brice
(1891-1951) knew early on that she
wanted to be a performer. With few
opportunities open to a child of Jewish
immigrants, she found her niche in
comedy. Brice made a name for herself
in Irving Berlin's Broadway show *The
College Girls.* Singing in a put-on
Yiddish accent, she brought the house
down. She later starred in the Ziegfeld
Follies and had a popular radio program
from 1938-1951, in which she played
Baby Snooks, a difficult and precocious
toddler.

Rosser Reeves Star Ruby

National Museum of Natural History
National Gem and Mineral Collection
Gift of Rosser Reeves

This magnificent gem is considered one of the largest and finest star rubies in the world. Donated by advertising mogul Rosser Reeves to the Smithsonian in 1965, the Sri Lankan stone is renowned for its rich color and well-defined star pattern. It weighs 138.7 carats. Reeves called the gem his "baby" and carried it with him for good luck.

Lunar Rocket

1969
Designed by Eddie Squires
Printed by Stead McAlpin & Co. for
Warner Fabrics
London, England
Screen printed in five colors on plain
woven cotton
Cooper-Hewitt, National Design Museum
Gift of Eddie Squires and Richard Reiche

On July 21, 1969, Neil Armstrong became
the first man to walk on the moon. That
year also saw the creation of this star-
studded textile design by Eddie Squires,
which incorporates parallel stripes of
rising *Saturn V* rockets with two images
of the *Apollo 9* capsule hovering near the
surface of the Earth and Moon. *Apollo
9* launched several months before the
moon landing mission. It was the first
manned demonstration of the lunar
module system's performance. The beauty
of space and the public excitement about
lunar exploration are reflected in this
textile from the Cooper-Hewitt, National
Design Museum.

Katharine Hepburn

1933
Edward Jean Steichen
Gelatin silver print
National Portrait Gallery,
Reprinted with Permission of
Joanna T. Steichen

Beneath the reflective pose taken
by Hepburn (1907-2003) in this
photograph by Edward Steichen was a
fiery heroine waiting to be unleashed.
Star of movies such as *The Philadelphia
Story, African Queen,* and *Guess Who's
Coming to Dinner,* Kate Hepburn was
known as a feisty co-star to actors
Cary Grant, James Stewart, Humphrey
Bogart, and Spencer Tracy. During
her career, which spanned more than
seventy years, she was nominated for
twelve Best Actress Oscars and won
four, the last in 1981 for *On Golden
Pond.*

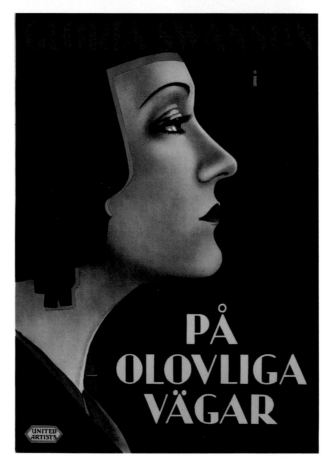

Gloria Swanson

1932
J. Olsens
Color lithographic poster
National Portrait Gallery

A star of the silent screen, Gloria Swanson (1897-1983) was a versatile performer, appearing in comedies as well as dramas, often as the romantic lead. Though barely five feet tall, she was, in her heyday, seen in extravagant outfits that were bedecked in jewels, beads, and ostrich or peacock feathers. When the "talkies" replaced silent films, Swanson's popularity declined. Ironically, one of her comeback roles was portraying a former silent movie star whose audience had forgotten her in *Sunset Boulevard*.

Ingrid Bergman

1948
Bernard Lancy
Color lithographic poster
National Portrait Gallery
™ 2007 Ingrid Bergman by CMG Worldwide, Inc.

Not only was actress Ingrid Bergman (1915–1982) a great star, she was also a convincing saint in the RKO film version of the life of Joan of Arc. The original poster for this 1948 movie, now in the collection of the National Portrait Gallery, depicts a likeness of Bergman posed before a stained glass window reminiscent of those in French cathedrals of the Middle Ages. She gazes skyward from the armored helmet, holding a sword, also pointing to the heavens.

53

Martha Graham

c. 1936
Sonya Noskowiak
Gelatin silver print
National Portrait Gallery
© The Estate of Sonya Noskowiak owned by
A.F. Noskowiak

Dancer and choreographer Martha
Graham (1894-1991) once said,
"No artist is ahead of his time. He
is his time." Certainly, not everyone
appreciated Graham's early work in
modern dance. When this portrait was
taken in 1936, during Graham's first
transcontinental tour with her company,
many audiences found her work too
avant-garde. But Graham persisted,
choreographing more than 180 works in
her long career and winning acceptance
for modern dance as a serious art form.
She performed on stage until she was
seventy-five years old.

Greta Garbo

The glamorous and mysterious film star Greta Garbo (1905-1990) was born in Sweden. She moved to the United States in 1925 to work for MGM, appearing in the silent film *The Torrent* in 1926. Through the thirties and forties, the seductive Garbo played many acclaimed roles and won four Oscar nominations. In 1941, at the age of thirty-six, she retired from acting. In 1954, she was awarded a special Oscar for past unforgettable performances.

All-Star Social Club

1944
Addison N. Scurlock
Gelatin silver print
Archives Center, National Museum of
American History
Scurlock Studio Collection

This "all-star" social club in Washington,
D.C., is from the Scurlock Studio
Collection in the Archives Center at
the National Museum of American
History. African American photographer
Addison Scurlock (1883-1964) opened
his own studio in 1911. He became a
respected professional in Washington's
segregated black community, recognized
for his fine studio portraits of celebrated
black entertainers and intellectuals. He
also documented the lives of African
American citizens and important events
in the black middle class community.
The American History museum has more
than 20,000 Scurlock photographs and
250,000 of his negatives.

Star-shaped Tile

Early 14th century
Islamic, Il-Khanid Dynasty
Stoneware, composite body
painted under clear glaze
Freer Gallery of Art
Museum purchase

This star-shaped architectural tile is
painted an almost celestial blue and
decorated with flowers and leaves.
Ceramics makers in the Islamic world
used colors and intricate designs to
animate very simple shapes. Drawing
on a variety of decorative sources, they
expanded their repertoire of calligraphic,
abstract, and figurative motifs.

Anne May Wong

1937
Nickolas Muray
Color cabro print
National Portrait Gallery
© Nickolas Muray Photo Archives

A true beauty, Anna May Wong made her film debut in 1919 as an extra in *The Red Lantern*. Soon she was Hollywood's leading Chinese American actress, but because of racial prejudice of the times was often relegated to minor roles while Caucasian actresses took the lead parts. In the film version of Pearl Buck's *The Good Earth,* Wong was passed over for the role of O-Lan in favor of Luise Rainer. When this photo was taken, Wong's film career was nearing its close.

1944
Harry Warnecke
Color carbro print
National Portrait Gallery
Gift of Elsie M. Warnecke
NY Daily News, © Daily News, LP
Image of Lucille Ball used with permission of
Desilu, too, LLC

The first episode of *I Love Lucy* debuted
on CBS in 1951. Soon audiences were
enjoying the foibles of the hilarious
red-headed housewife, Lucy Ricardo,
her bandleader husband, Ricky, and
their daffy neighbors, Ethel and Fred
Mertz. Ball's comic brilliance won the
show the No. 1 rating on TV for four
of its six seasons. Ball's expressive face
and famous slapstick routines live on in
re-runs. This lovely color image of Ball
was taken by Harry Warnecke for the
Daily News.

Myrna Loy

c. 1940
Wladyslaw Theodore Benda
Molded paper mask
National Portrait Gallery

Myrna Williams (1905-1993), the
daughter of a rancher, made her stage
debut at age twelve, and taking the
stage name "Myrna Loy," became
a star of the screen. This mask was
made when she was at the height
of her career. In a contest two years
before, she had been voted "Queen of
Hollywood." Loy is best remembered for
her role as Nora Charles in the movie
The Thin Man.

1918
Sven Brasch
Printer: Ihrich
Linocut poster
National Portrait Gallery

One of the great actors of the silent film era, Charlie Chaplin was best known for his character "The Tramp," a vagrant who had the manners and affect of a gentleman down to the bowler hat and cane. Wearing a tightly buttoned coat and oversized pants and shoes, the Tramp's sad face and odd antics made him a hit with audiences throughout the world. Chaplin's great films—including *City Lights* and *Modern Times*—are classics.

WORLD CIRKUS — CINEMA VARIETÉ

23.-31. December
hver Aften Kl. 7½

CHAPLIN
SOM GREVE
Komisk Farce i 2 Akter

Varieté-Afdeling:
Johnsen & Johnsen
Komisk Jonglør

Kay Whitt
International excentrick

Verdensspejlet
i Film

HANS
ÆGTESKAB
SKUESPIL I 5 AKTER
MED
NORMA TALMADGE
i Hovedrollen

Hver Søndag Eftm. Kl. 4:
Folkeforestilling
Smaa Priser

Buster Keaton

c. 1928
Jean Albert Mercier
Color lithographic poster
National Portrait Gallery

John Frank Keaton, Jr. (1895-1966),
known as "Buster," was a popular silent
film star, comic actor, and filmmaker. In
this colorful poster, he is seen behind
the camera rather than in front of it.
Keaton began performing in vaudeville
at the age of three. Later he worked
on early films with Roscoe "Fatty"
Arbuckle and eventually had his own
production unit, Buster Keaton Studios.
His more famous feature films include
Our Hospitality (1923), *The Navigator*
(1924), *The Cameraman* (1928) or
L'Operateur in French, for which this
poster was created, and his most
enduring, *The General* (1927).

63

Kermit the Frog

Can a frog be a star? Yes—if the frog is
Kermit, the lovable Muppet character
from the TV show *Sesame Street*.
Created as a hand and rod puppet by
Jim Henson in 1955, Kermit took on
many human roles—as comic, master of
ceremonies, and crusader for tolerance.
His hit song "It's Not Easy Being Green"
addressed the issue of differences
(ethnic and racial) for kids. Kermit is
a popular exhibit at the Smithsonian's
National Museum of American History.

Sirius A and B: A Double-Star System in the Constellation Canis Major

1999
X-ray
Smithsonian Astrophysical Observatory
Chandra X-ray Observatory
White Dwarfs and Planetary Nebulas
Collection

The Sirius star system is located 8.6 light years from Earth. In this image, the bright light source is from Sirius B, a white dwarf star that produces very low-energy X-rays. Sirius A is a normal star, twice as massive as the sun and ten times the size of Sirius B. But here Sirius A is seen only as a dim source of light, possibly because ultraviolet radiation from it leaked through the filter on the detector of the Chandra X-ray telescope at the Smithsonian's Astrophysical Observatory.

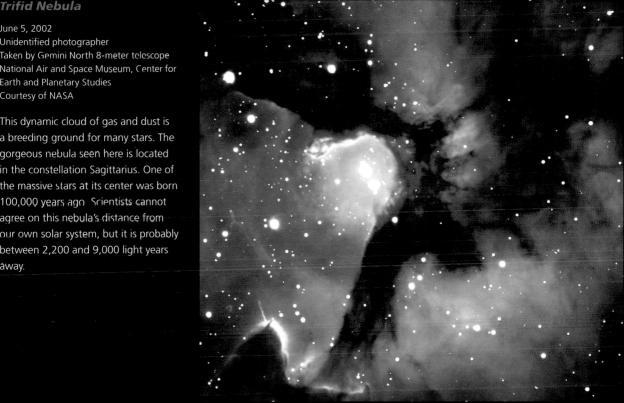

Trifid Nebula

June 5, 2002
Unidentified photographer
Taken by Gemini North 8-meter telescope
National Air and Space Museum, Center for
Earth and Planetary Studies
Courtesy of NASA

This dynamic cloud of gas and dust is
a breeding ground for many stars. The
gorgeous nebula seen here is located
in the constellation Sagittarius. One of
the massive stars at its center was born
100,000 years ago. Scientists cannot
agree on this nebula's distance from
our own solar system, but it is probably
between 2,200 and 9,000 light years
away.

Jessye Norman, New York, 1983

1983
Irving Penn
Platinum-palladium print
National Portrait Gallery
Gift of Irving Penn
Copyright © 1983 by Condé Nast
Publications, Inc.

Jessye Norman's (b. 1945) lustrous voice made the soprano a star shortly after her graduation from college. This photo by Irving Penn, which appeared in *Vanity Fair* magazine in 1983, shows her preparing for her debut at the Metropolitan Opera, where she would perform the role of Cassandra in Hector Berlioz's *Les Troyens* for the Met's hundredth anniversary season. An experienced performer who had sung in the greatest opera houses throughout the world, Norman confessed that her Met debut made her so nervous, she "turned to jelly."

Mae West

1935
C. Kenneth Lobben
Gelatin silver print
National Portrait Gallery
Gift of Keith de Lellis

Famous for her suggestive one-liners
("Come up and see me sometime."),
Mae West (1893-1980) was earthy, sexy,
and risqué. This photograph is one of
the publicity shots for her film *Goin' to
Town*. Because West had had trouble
with Hollywood censors in the past, the
film was cleaned up a bit. Sadly, it was
a disappointment for West's fans, who
enjoyed her bawdiness and found the
movie bland and boring.

71

Credits

Smithsonian image numbers are followed by names of the photographers, when known.

p. 2 digital
p. 3 NPG.93.119
p. 5 digital, NMAH
p. 7 72.313 A-B
p. 8 1981-29-511 by Matt Flynn
p. 9 A-04-04-39
p. 10 digital, NMAH
p. 11 91-10686 by Robert Lautman
p. 13 2002-8037
p. 14 AC0300-0000015
p. 15 AC0300-0000069
p. 16 digital, NMAH
p. 17 NPG.82.66
p. 18 digital, NMAH
p. 19 2005-36186
p. 20 0300600274
p. 23 NPG.97.177
p. 24 2005-24677
p. 25 NPG.93.101
p. 26 AC0300-0000067
p. 27 AC0300-0000068
p. 28 NPG.98.80
p. 29 86.929
p. 30 1986.65.351
p. 31 261056

p. 32 NPG.93.153
p. 33 NASM-2B30439-P
p. 34 SIL-1-28-Calkins
p. 36 SI-86-147
p. 37 SI-94-6307
p. 38 NASM-A-336
p. 39 NPG.99.5
p. 40 2004-20304
p. 41 2004-11265 by Eric Long
p. 42 1997.108.28
p. 43 AAA-kurtchar-8090
p. 44 72.144
p. 46 S2003.8.2061
p. 47 NPG.94.6
p. 48 95-40275
p. 49 1991-102-1 by Dennis Cowley
p. 50 NPG.2000.61
p. 52 NPG.97.143
p. 53 NPG.97.47
p. 54 NPG.94.96
p. 55 NPG.91.210
p. 56 618ns 0178898-01
p. 57 F1999.12
p. 58 NPG.99.45
p. 59 NPG.94.40

p. 61 T/NPG.93.123.03
p. 62 NPG.93.119
p. 63 NPG.86.170
p. 64 digital
p. 66 0065_xray (_Sirius_A&B)
p. 67 trifid_gemini
p. 69 S/NPG.88.70.39
p. 71 NPG.95.119

Cover: *Ray Charles Sunglasses*
National Museum of American History
Division of Music, Sports, and Entertainment

Prince's Yellow Cloud Guitar
1989
National Museum of American History
Division of Music, Sports, and Entertainment
Gift of Paisley Park Enterprises